150 Ways to Keep Your Job

Nancy Lobb
illustrated by Michael Waterman

Cover photography by © The Terry Wild Studio

1 2 3 4 5 6 7 8 9 10

ISBN 0-8251-2473-5

Copyright © 1994
J. Weston Walch, Publisher
P. O. Box 658 • Portland, Maine 04104-0658

Printed in the United States of America

Contents

Introduction .... *v*

Pullout Section:

   Vocabulary .... *ix*

   Answer Key .... *xi*

Chapter 1. The First Day on the Job 1

Chapter 2. Looking Right on the Job 9
   Using Good Grooming 11
   Dressing Right for Work 16

Chapter 3. Getting Along with Your Boss 19

Chapter 4. Getting Along with Your Co-workers 28
   Being Part of the Team 29
   Friends at Work 33
   Danger in the Workplace 36

Chapter 5. Doing Your Best Work 39

Chapter 6. Communication Skills 46
   Speaking Skills 47
   Listening Skills 48
   Using the Telephone at Work 52
   Dealing with Customers 56

Chapter 7. Problems at Work 60
   Stress at Work 60
   Discrimination 62
   Sexual Harassment 64
   Romance in the Office 66
   The Office Party 67
   Crime in the Workplace 69
   Quitting Your Job 70

    Getting Fired or Laid Off 73

Chapter 8. Getting Promotions and Raises **79**
    Getting a Promotion 79
    How to Get a Raise 84

Summary: 150 Ways to Keep Your Job **88**

Introduction

Finding a job can be tough. Some people are lucky. They have friends or family they can work for. Or they can be in "the right place at the right time." They find out about a job without looking. But most of us have to look for a job. This can take time. It can be frustrating. Here are some ways to make your job hunt easier:

Find the job that's right for you.

- List your skills. Then think of the kinds of jobs you could do and would like to do.

- Ask parents, teachers, and guidance counselors about jobs that might suit you.

- Remember, the best way to keep a job is to find a job that you like and that you can do well.

- Don't panic and take the first job you are offered! You may regret it later.

Where to look:

- The want ads are a good place to start. But many other people are reading the same ads and applying for the same jobs.

- Try a local employment agency. They often have listings that are not in the newspaper.

- Find out about companies where people enjoy their work. Call the personnel departments at those companies to set up an appointment for an interview.

- But the best way to find work is to tell *everybody* you know that you are looking for a job. Let people know what kind of work you want to do.

- Don't be shy! Jobs rarely come looking for you. You have to get out there and work to find the job that's right for you.

- And don't get discouraged. The time you spend finding the right job will be worth it in the end.

Imagine you are the boss of a large company. You employ many workers to do a number of different jobs. Some of these workers will be valuable to the company. You will probably keep these workers. Others will not work out, and you will have to fire them.

How can a worker make sure to be in the first group: those who keep their jobs and get pay raises and promotions? What does it take to make a boss happy, to fit in with other workers, and in short, to be a good worker?

Many researchers have studied this question. Their answers may surprise you. Here are the top 10 gripes bosses have about their workers:

1. Poor grooming habits
2. Unsuitable or sloppy clothing
3. Dishonesty
4. Wasting time
5. Being late to work
6. Missing too much work
7. Not following directions or company rules
8. Complaining to co-workers about the job
9. Laziness
10. Not caring about doing a good job

What does this list tell us about keeping a job? It all comes down to two things: *appearance* and *attitude*. In other words, what really matters is how you look and how you act.

Bosses want their workers to be neat, clean, and dressed right for the job. And bosses value a good attitude toward the job.

You can learn many work skills in school or by on-the-job training. You may learn how to type, how to use tools, or how to file. But these skills alone will not be enough to allow you to KEEP THAT JOB!

In addition to your work skills, you need to have the skills listed in this book. *150 Ways to Keep Your Job* will tell you:

- How to handle the first day on a job
- How to be well groomed and dressed right for the job
- How to get along with your boss
- How to get along with your co-workers
- How to deal with customers
- How to do your best work
- How to improve your speaking and listening skills
- How to handle serious problems at work
- How to get raises and promotions
- and much more.

When you finish *150 Ways to Keep Your Job*, you'll know what it takes to KEEP THAT JOB!

Vocabulary

Introduction

promotion	appearance	customer	pay raise
attitude	co-worker	well groomed	

Chapter 1: The First Day on the Job

cooperate	pleasant	suitable	good-natured
consequences	balanced diet	probationary period	

Chapter 2: Looking Right on the Job

deodorant	cologne	casual clothes
posture	confidence	clothing fads
dressy clothes		

Chapter 3: Getting Along with Your Boss

mechanic	criticism	loyal	privately
control	responsible	dependable	
positive attitude			

Chapter 4: Getting Along with Co-Workers

conflicts	respect	gossip	respectful
disagree	polite	situation	complain
handicapped	ignore	considerate	

Chapter 5: Doing Your Best Work

ability	reliable	negative attitude
effort	success	handicap

Chapter 6: Communication Skills

communication	customer	interrupt	slang
compliment	apology	eye contact	on hold
introduced	message	on commission	complaint

(continued)

Chapter 7: Problems at Work

stress	relaxation	sexual harassment
victim	succeed	good impression
discrimination	union	personnel department
lawyer	severance pay	unemployment compensation
recommendation	Civil Right Act	

Equal Employment Opportunity Commission (EEOC)
American Civil Liberties Union (ACLU)

Chapter 8: Getting Promotions and Raises

promotion	goals	adult education
dependable	responsibility	

Answer Key

Chapter 1: The First Day on the Job

■ "Right or Wrong?" ■

1. right
2. wrong
3. wrong
4. right
5. wrong
6. right
7. right
8. right
9. wrong
10. wrong
11. right
12. wrong
13. right
14. wrong

■ "What Do You Think?" ■

(Answers will vary.) Possible answers:

1. On the job and at school you should be on time, do your best work, be friendly to others, respect your boss (teacher), be willing to learn, and observe unwritten rules of conduct.

2. Consequences of poor work on the job are more severe. On the job you may be fired for not measuring up. Most bosses will not put up with poor conduct or performance. On the plus side, you earn money on the job.

3. It is up to you to be sure you learn to do your job well. You will probably have someone assigned to help you. But it is up to you to ask questions, study, and be willing to learn.

4. It is up to you to get along with your boss and co-workers. If some of them are hard to get along with, you must still make up your mind that you will be the one to go the extra mile.

5. The new worker must follow hints 1–10. You should be very careful to have a great attitude and to make sure your appearance is good. You should be willing to learn and to do your best work.

■ "What Are the Consequences?" ■

1. At school: You get a low grade.
   At work: You get reprimanded or fired.

2. At school: You get a low grade.
   At work: You get reprimanded or fired.

3. At school: You are marked tardy.
   At work: Your pay is docked.

4. At school: Your grades might be lower.
   At work: You get fired.

5. At school: You could get a lower grade. You might have to stay up late to finish it.
   At work: You may do a poor job and be fired.

6. At school: Nothing; poorer grades.
   At work: You might be fired.

7. At school: You get better grades.
   At work: You might get a raise or promotion.

Chapter 2: Looking Right on the Job

■ "You're the Boss!" ■

(Answers will vary.) Possible answers:

1. People like stores where they buy food to be especially clean. If store and restaurant workers are not clean and neat, people will buy their food elsewhere.

2. Many customers will think that if a salesperson isn't able to keep himself clean and presentable, he probably doesn't know what he's talking about either.

3. A barber who can't keep herself clean doesn't appear to have the ability to help the customer look good either.

4. The other workers may avoid someone who is dirty/messy.

■ "Problem on the Job" ■

(Answers will vary.) Possible answers:

5. Hamid thought that as long as no customers saw him, he could come to work looking any way he wanted to. He was wrong because his appearance still affected his boss and co-workers. His poor grooming sent the message that he did not care about himself or his job enough to try and look presentable.

6. Yes. Three years is a long time.

7. Hamid should get over being embarrassed and be thankful he knows the problem. He should go ahead and clean up his act.

■ "Right or Wrong?" ■

1. no
2. yes
3. no
4. no
5. no
6. no
7. yes
8. yes
9. yes

Chapter 3: Getting Along with the Boss

■ "Can You Get Along with the Boss?" ■

1. a
2. b
3. c
4. a
5. c
6. c
7. c
8. b
9. a
10. a
11. a

■ "Who's in Control?" ■

(Answers will vary.) Possible answers:

1. A lot. Have a positive attitude and look for the bright side in what you are doing.

2. A lot. Make up your mind you will get along with your boss, even if she makes that difficult.

3. A lot. You must do your share of the work and try to get along with the others.

4. A lot. Doing your best work, having a pleasant appearance and attitude will go a long way.

5. A lot. Make up your mind to do the best you can at whatever you are assigned.

6. A lot. Follow the hints in this chapter.

7. A lot. Do your best at the jobs you are assigned now. More interesting and responsible jobs will follow.

8. A lot. You must consistently do your best work and be on time.

■ "Handling Criticism" ■

(Answers will vary.) Possible answers:

1. I'm sorry. I will do better from now on.
2. I'm sorry. I'll be more careful to be on time.
3. I'm sorry. I will be sure to eat between 1 and 2.
4. I'm sorry. I will go back right now to those stops and make it right. It won't happen again.
5. I'm sorry. I will reread the dress code and be sure to follow it.

Chapter 4: Getting Along with Your Co-workers

■ "Can You Get Along with Your Co-workers?" ■

1. a
2. b
3. b
4. a
5. a
6. b

■ "Yes or No?" ■

1. no
2. no
3. no
4. yes
5. no
6. yes

■ "How Do You Rate?" ■

(Answers will vary.)

■ "What Would You Do?" ■

(Answers will vary.) Possible answers:

1. Try to be friendly to others. Follow the hints in this chapter.
2. Ask her how you can help. Offer to babysit her children. Take food to her family, etc.
3. Find another place to smoke.
4. Keep it to yourself.
5. Don't brag. Tell your speed if you are asked.
6. Tell the friend you are out of money. If the friend offers to lend you some, you should pay it back as soon as possible. Don't ask to borrow money. You might suggest going to lunch after you're paid instead.
7. Stay out of it.
8. Congratulate the other person. Keep your hurt feelings to yourself.

■ "Do you Agree?" ■

(Answers will vary.) Possible answers:

1. Yes. You are hired to do a job. That is your most important obligation. But you need to get along with the others too.
2. No. Do make friends at work. They can make the job more fun. It will also make working together easier and help you do a better job.
3. No. You can have friends at work. But you don't have to spend that much time with them outside of work.
4. No. You do want to make friends. But choose your friends slowly, as you get to know everyone better.
5. Yes. If you are a good friend, others will like you.
6. No. There's a good chance that whatever you say will get back to your boss.

7. No. Arguing in a calm and reasonable way makes you look much better.

Chapter 5: Doing Your Best Work

■ "Your Work Habits" ■

(Answers will vary.)

■ "Be Positive!" ■

(Answers will vary.) Possible answers:

1. The company is not getting what it's paying for. You don't have the pride of a job done well.

2. You may be missing the opportunity for advancing to a better job if you perform poorly on a lower job. Any job you accept is worthy of your best effort. And, just because a job is not important to you, that doesn't mean it's not important to the company.

3. Leaving a mess is not being considerate. It makes others angry if they have to clean up behind you. And in some cases, it could make your workplace unsafe.

4. You will feel good if you really know your job. The company benefits from your added expertise.

5. When you put off jobs they become an irritation in the back of your mind. Your boss may become annoyed if you take too long finishing a job.

6. You can't learn if you don't ask questions. An informed worker is a better worker.

7. Everyone makes mistakes. If you don't keep trying, you can't learn from your mistakes.

8. If you are late completing a job, you may hold up other projects that need to be done.

9. No one should be ashamed of an honest job. Do your best, even if it is a low level job. You may be able to work

your way up to something else later. All jobs are important in keeping a company working smoothly.

■ "What Do You Think?" ■

(Answers will vary.) Possible answers:

1. All the hints listed in this chapter are important. Doing good, reliable work with a good attitude is the key.

2. If you enjoy your work, you will be more careful to do it right. You probably have a good attitude as well.

3. If you have a handicap, the first step is to accept that fact and move past it to do your best with the situation you have.

4. All jobs, and the people who do them well, are important to a smooth-running company.

5. Try, try again. Don't expect to be perfect. Learn from your mistakes and give it another try.

6. The best way to handle mistakes is to admit them and try to learn from them. Blaming others makes you look bad.

7. A positive attitude allows you to make friends more easily, learn from others more easily, correct mistakes more easily, and learn your job better.

Chapter 6: Communication Skills

■ "What Do You Think?" ■

(Answers will vary.) Possible answers:

1. a. A boss who doesn't listen is losing the chance to learn a lot of valuable information about procedures that need improving, morale problems, and so on.

   b. A salesperson who doesn't listen won't understand what the customer really wants. So sales will suffer.

c. A worker who doesn't listen won't get along well with his co-workers.

2. Because most people like to talk. But not as many are really good listeners. And without listening no communication can take place.

■ "Do You Agree?" ■

(Answers will vary.) Possible answers:

1. Disagree. Maintaining eye contact makes you look interested in what the other person is saying.
2. Disagree. Interrupting is never O.K. unless it is an emergency. And then say, "Excuse me for interrupting, but… ."
3. Disagree. Accept the compliment and say "thank you."
4. Disagree. Apologize promptly.
5. Disagree. Generally you should do whatever your boss asks, but not if it goes against the law or your moral beliefs.
6. Disagree. Many people are offended by 4-letter words. This language makes you look crude, not mature.
7. Disagree. Get the name straight right off. Ask for it to be repeated if necessary.
8. Disagree. Taking notes is a good way to be sure to get all the instructions right.
9. Disagree. Learn as much as you can about the company *and* your own job.
10. Disagree. It's true that people may like to listen to you, but they won't trust you either.

■ "Problem Callers" ■

(Answers will vary.) Possible answers:

1. Remain polite. Offer to take a message and have the boss return the call. Hang up if the caller becomes abusive. Later, report the incident to your boss.

2. Take the caller's name and phone number and offer to call back as soon as you can.

3. Remain polite. Tell the person you cannot make an appointment without the information. Report the call to the dentist later.

4. Tell the caller what items were charged if you have that information. If not, take the caller's name and number and refer the call to a manager.

5. Apologize to the boss. Try to improve your grammar and speech by taking a speech class. Or you could read a book about good speaking habits. Poor grammar and sloppy speech will hold you back in your work, so do what you can to improve.

■ "Do You Agree?" ■

(Answers will vary.) Possible answers:

1. Agree. Customers in the store shouldn't be kept waiting while you talk on the phone. If you can't end the call, quickly get the number and return the call later.

2. Disagree. Treat the customer with respect. You should know more about your product than the customer. But that doesn't mean the customer is not intelligent. People resent being talked down to.

3. Agree. If you look businesslike, your appearance backs up your words.

4. Disagree. Treat customer complaints carefully. If the customer is wrong, first agree with the feelings he is expressing ("I see why you were unhappy.") Correct the situation by offering a refund, replacement, etc.

5. Disagree. In the long run a company will make more money by being honest with their customers.

6. Agree. A good salesperson makes the customer feel glad she came into the store.

7. Agree. The customer may not always be right, but a smart company values its customers and treats them well.

Chapter 7: Problems at Work

■ "What Do You Think?" ■

(Answers will vary.) Possible answers:

1. NO. It sounds as if Dana overreacted. The boss probably should not have hugged her. But if she objected, she could have said so tactfully.
2. YES. This is the polite thing to do.
3. NO. If she really hates it, she could tactfully remind her boss that they are "women," not "girls."
4. NO. Not eating properly will cause more problems. Ford will be low on energy before the day is over.
5. YES. There's a time for work and a time for romance.
6. NO. Mario is stealing from the shop unless the boss gives him permission.
7. NO. Hanna should not quit her job for an uncertain one.
8. YES. This way Ferdo can learn from his mistakes and do better next time.

■ "What Would You Do?" ■

(Answers will vary.) Possible answers:

1. "When you say things like that, it makes me very uncomfortable. I would like you to stop."
2. Go anyway and act as if you're enjoying it.
3. Do the very best job you can. Make an effort to learn your job well. Be reliable about getting to work on time and finishing your work on time.

4. Make time for exercise or a hobby you enjoy. Be sure to eat well and get enough sleep. If this doesn't help, you might look for another, less stressful job.

5. If others tease you, just laugh along with them. But keep your romantic relationship out of the workplace.

6. Tell the co-worker in private that she could get herself in trouble. Tell the boss if the stealing continues or is on a large scale.

7. Cool down. Take a while to think about it and let things get back to normal.

8. Definitely. Ask the boss for whatever benefits you think you should get.

■ "What Does It Mean?" ■

(Answers will vary.) Possible answers:

1. Office parties are a part of your job. You shouldn't get wild and crazy there any more than you would at work.

2. Discrimination still exists even though it is against the law.

3. If your body is in top shape, you can more easily handle whatever comes your way.

4. You're not paid to have a romance. You're paid to work.

5. No job is without its problems.

6. If you behave poorly when fired, you won't be able to count on your old company for a good reference or for another job in the future.

Chapter 8: Getting Promotions and Raises

■ "Right or Wrong?" ■

1. right	5. wrong	9. right	13. right
2. right	6. wrong	10. right	14. wrong
3. wrong	7. wrong	11. right	15. wrong
4. right	8. right	12. right	

■ "Will You Get Ahead on the Job?" ■

(Answers will vary.)

■ "Will This Person Get a Raise?" ■

(Answers will vary.) Possible answers:

1. YES. Carly will be able to prove why she deserves a raise.
2. NO. The boss may not be in a good mood at 7:30 Monday morning. Let the boss pick the time for the meeting.
3. NO. The boss doesn't want to hear all that. Paula should focus on why she deserves a raise.
4. YES. It's O.K. to remind the boss as long as you don't make a pest of yourself.
5. NO. If he finds out why he didn't get the raise, maybe he can improve in some area and later get the raise.
6. YES. Cora is showing the boss why she is worth more money to the company now than when she was hired.
7. NO. The boss may tell her to go ahead and quit.
8. NO. Aaron hasn't done anything special to deserve a raise. Workers are expected to be at work every day.
9. NO. It's best not to ask for a raise in bad times.
10. NO. Julie is making a pest of herself.

Chapter 1

The First Day on the Job

As you enter the world of work on your first job, you may feel like a stranger in a strange land. Don't worry. This won't last long. But, it's important to start off right! The way you start a job will affect how well you get along with your boss and the other workers.

Chances are you'll be a bit nervous about starting a new job. You know you want to do well. But you're not sure if you know what to do. You may be worried about whether the boss or the other workers will like you. You may wonder if you have the skills to do the work. The best way to feel more sure of yourself is to be ready for things that are likely to come up on the job. And that's what *150 Ways to Keep Your Job!* is all about.

Get started on the right foot! Here are 10 ways to start out right and KEEP YOUR JOB

1. Get to work on time.

You should always be on time. But it's doubly important the first day. Give it a trial run ahead of time. Be sure you know how to get there and how long it will take. Double check bus or subway schedules. Then allow plenty of time to get yourself ready. Leave home a little earlier than you think you need to. If you have allowed yourself too much time, take a walk and get to know the neighborhood you'll be working in. Try not to arrive at your new job more than 5 or 10 minutes early.

2. Ask your boss what he or she would like to be called.

Say "Should I call you Ms./Mr. _____ ?" Don't call the boss by his or her first name unless asked to do so.

3. Introduce yourself to your co-workers.

Be pleasant and smile. Learn their names as soon as you can.

4. Show that you are willing to learn.

Cooperate with co-workers who offer to show you the ropes. Ask questions. Listen carefully to what you're told. Take notes if you need to.

5. Go all out to do your best work.

No matter what tasks you are given, do your best. As the new kid on the block, you are likely to get some simple or boring chores. Don't complain.

6. Find out the *unwritten rules* of your workplace.

These rules are ways to act that everyone else knows, but no one will think of spelling out for you. Look around you to find out:

What kind of clothing is suitable?

How loud/quiet should you be?

How neat should you try to be?

Can you eat/drink at your work station?

How should you act at lunch/coffee breaks?

Can you take or make personal phone calls?

It's important to remember, however, that just because you see another worker doing something, that doesn't mean it's OK. The best thing to do is *ask*. You should also remember that it's best to use good judgment. Other workers may wear sloppy clothes or eat at their work stations. But your boss may not like it.

7. Take "newcomer" jokes or pranks in stride.

Sometimes workers will play jokes or tricks on a new person. They may give you a job no one else wants, like cleaning up a mess or making coffee. Or you might be assigned the worst shift to work. This kind of thing is normal. The others are testing you to see how you'll fit in. If you're good natured about it, it shouldn't last long. (Of course, if you're asked to do something that is dangerous or against the law, you shouldn't go along with it. If that happens, walk away and inform the boss.)

8. Be friendly to everyone.

But don't be too friendly too fast. You could find out too late that you've become chums with someone who's on the outs with the boss. Or someone who is about to lose her job for poor work habits. It's best to get to know everyone a little better before you get too close to anyone.

9. Give the job a fair chance.

If the going seems tough, don't take the easy way out. Give yourself and the job a fair chance. If things still seem to be going badly, talk it over with the boss.

10. Eat a balanced diet and get enough sleep.

Starting a new job is hard work! Be good to yourself. If you're rested and are not hungry, things are bound to go better!

■ *RIGHT OR WRONG?* ■

Read what each of these workers did on their first day on the job. Write **Right** or **Wrong** by each action.

_____ 1. Lyle tried to learn his co-workers' names right away.

_____ 2. Danny wanted to be friendly. So he called his boss "Joe."

_____ 3. Clark skipped breakfast to get to work on time. He ate a snack when he got to work.

_____ 4. Maria went over the directions for each task she had to do. Then she asked questions about everything she didn't understand.

_____ 5. Lily was sure she already knew how to do her new job. So she told her co-workers "no thanks!" when they offered to show her the ropes.

_____ 6. Ken noticed some of the other workers had soft drinks at their desks. So he felt free to do so also.

_____ 7. Cara noticed her boss was very neat and favored employees who turned in neat work. So she knew she'd have to try to be neat too.

_____ 8. Liza's co-workers gave her the worst jobs to do. She thought they might be just testing her. She didn't say anything, since she was new.

_____ 9. Bill's co-workers sent him all over the building looking for a left-handed hammer. When he found out it was a joke, he got mad so they'd know not to fool around with him.

_____ 10. Marcie wasn't sure if it was O.K. to leave the building on her lunch break. She needed to do some errands, so she left quietly by the back door so no one would notice.

_____ 11. LaToya arrived at work 10 minutes early the first day. She had allowed herself more time than she really needed.

_____ 12. Raol invited all his co-workers to his place for a beer after his first day on the job.

_____ 13. Lane's co-workers offered her drugs during break time. She refused even though they teased her.

_____ 14. Mark couldn't read well. He was told to read the instructions, then repair a machine. Mark was afraid to say he couldn't read well enough to understand what to do. So he went ahead and tried to do the job anyway.

■ *What Do You Think?* ■

1. Name two ways a job and school are alike.

   _____

   _____

2. Name two ways they are different.

   _____

   _____

3. Whose responsibility is it to see that you learn to do your new job well? Why?

   _____

   _____

4. Whose responsibility is it to see that you get along with your boss and your co-workers? Why?

   _____

   _____

5. Most companies have a *probationary* period for new workers. This is a time to see if the new worker can do the job and fit in. A worker who does poorly during this time will be fired. What do

you think would be the most important things you should do to succeed in the probationary period?

_____

_____

■ *WHAT ARE THE CONSEQUENCES?* ■

Write the consequences for each action at work and at school.

Action	**At School**	**At Work**
1. You don't finish work you're assigned.		
2. You make several mistakes in your work.		
3. You arrive an hour late.		
4. You can't get along with your teacher (boss).		
5. You put your work off until the last minute.		

(continued)

Action	At School	At Work
6. You don't take anything very seriously.		
7. You take pride in doing your best work.		

Chapter 2

Looking Right on the Job

Looking right for work can help you succeed on the job. If you look sloppy, others might think your work will be sloppy too.

It's not fair! It's just not right! But it's true! Bosses and co-workers *do* judge you by how you look. Paying attention to your grooming and dress will help you KEEP THAT JOB!

Amy and Maria were hired as file clerks on the same day. Of the two, Amy had the better filing skills and some job experience as well. Maria knew just a little about filing. But she was a careful worker and was learning on the job.

Maria had very few clothes. But she kept them clean and pressed. She was neat and well groomed, too.

Amy did not think her appearance mattered since no customers saw her. She often arrived at work late, rushing in the door looking as though she'd just climbed out of bed. Her clothes were wrinkled and sometimes dirty. Her hair wasn't clean or combed. Upon arriving at work, she'd head straight for the ladies' room, where she put on lots of makeup and perfume to try and clean herself up.

The day came when the boss had to lay off some workers. Maria kept her job. But Amy was one of the first to go. Although she could do the work, she was not a credit to the company or herself. Her careless appearance cost her the job.

Using Good Grooming

Here are 9 things you should keep in mind if you want to be well groomed.

> **11. Keep yourself clean.**

Take a bath, shower, or sponge bath *every day.* Soap and water will rid your body of dirt, oil, germs, and odor.

> **12. Put on clean underwear and socks every day.**

> **13. Use a deodorant to help control body odor.**

But remember, a deodorant can't take the place of daily washing.

> **14. If you use cologne or aftershave, use only a little.**

Strong smells may offend others at work or irritate their allergies.

> **15. Keep your hair clean and trimmed.**

> **16. Make sure your hands are clean and your nails are trimmed.**

Make sure nail polish, if any, is neat and not too loud for work.

> **17. Keep your teeth clean and your breath fresh.**

Floss and brush twice a day.

> **18. Women should use makeup sparingly.**

Makeup that is put on neatly can look very nice. But if it's sloppy or if you use too much, it looks tacky.

> **19. Men, keep your moustache or beard clean and well trimmed.**

If you don't have a beard, make sure you shave as often as you need to in order to look neat.

Remember, it's important to look your best at work. Knowing you are well groomed will make you feel more sure of yourself at work. And that feeling of confidence will help you KEEP THAT JOB!

■ *CHECK YOURSELF OUT* ■

Pretend you are now on your job. Are you well groomed *right now* for your job?

Think about your grooming in the last 24 hours. Mark an X under YES or NO for each item listed below.

	YES	NO
1. I took a bath, shower, or sponge bath in the last 24 hours.		
2. I used a deodorant today.		
3. My hair is neat, clean, and trimmed.		
4. My face and hands are clean.		
5. My fingernails are clean and well shaped.		
6. I brushed and flossed my teeth last night.		

(continued)

	YES	NO
7. I brushed my teeth this morning.		
8. My clothes are neat and clean.		
9. I put on clean underwear and socks today.		
10. My shoes are clean and/or polished.		
11. I used only a little or no cologne or aftershave.		
12. My clothes look and feel good on me.		
13. I used good posture today.		
14. Women only: I used just a little or no makeup.		
15. Women only: My nail polish is not chipped, or I am not wearing nail polish.		
16. Men only: I shaved if needed to, or I kept my beard or mustache trimmed and clean.		
17. I like the way I look today.		

If you were starting a new job today, how would you need to improve your grooming?

■ You're the Boss! ■

Some bosses were talking about problems they had with their workers. Tell why you think each statement below was made.

1. *A grocery store manager:*
   "Poorly groomed checkers and baggers cause my store to lose customers."

   _____
   _____

2. *A manager of a used car lot:*
   "A poorly groomed salesperson cannot win the trust of the customer."

   _____
   _____

3. *The owner of a barber shop:*
   "A barber who is poorly groomed will get little walk-in business."

   _____
   _____

4. *An office manager:*
   "A secretary who is poorly groomed will not get along well with the other workers."

   _____
   _____

■ Problem on the Job ■

> Hamid worked in the mail room. He had worked there 3 years with no raise or promotion. When he asked his boss why, the answer was that his poor grooming and sloppy dress did not reflect well on the company.

5. Why do you think Hamid overlooked the importance of good grooming for working in the mail room? Why was he wrong?

   _____

   _____

6. Do you think Hamid's boss should have told him about the problem sooner?

   _____

   _____

(continued)

7. Hamid is embarrassed and a little angry. What do you think he should do now?

_____

_____

Dressing Right for Work

There is a lot of truth in the saying: "Dress for success!" Wearing suitable clothes that are neat and clean can go a long way toward making you look like a good employee.

Here are 8 sure-fire ways to dress right for work:

20. Dress as your co-workers dress.

Notice the sorts of clothes they wear and dress as they do, neither more casually nor more dressy.

21. Avoid wearing clothing fads to work.

Don't come to work decked out in all the latest clothing fads (unless you work in a place where that is suitable, like a clothing store). Buy classic clothes of good fabric that will last.

22. Learn to choose clothes that fit well.

Avoid clothing that is too tight or too loose.

23. Buy work clothes that are easy to take care of.

When you buy new clothes for work, keep in mind how much care they will need to keep looking right. If you don't want to iron, choose clothes that look good without ironing.

24. Wear simple jewelry, if any.

Don't wear jewelry that makes noise—bracelets that bang together, for example.

25. Be sure your clothes are neat and clean.

Keep everything clean: clothes, shoes, purse, briefcase, and wallet.

26. Have good posture.

Whatever you choose to wear will look better if you have good posture. Even the nicest clothes won't look good if you slouch and slump. Stand tall and carry yourself with pride.

27. Try to always look your best at work.

Look at yourself in the mirror before you leave for work. Do you look suitable for your job? Do you like the way you look?

■ *Right or Wrong?* ■

Write **YES** by each statement that tells a good way to dress for work. Write **NO** by each statement that does not.

_____ 1. Sally was hired to sell makeup in a department store. She wore no makeup and dressed in jeans.

_____ 2. Sam saw that all the other baggers wore jeans and T-shirts to work. So he dressed that way too.

_____ 3. Jennings noticed that her blouse smelled a little, but it still looked clean and pressed. She decided she could wear it one more day.

_____ 4. Mark kept his clothes clean and pressed. But his shoes were scuffed and dirty.

(continued)

_____ 5. Sue had a job as a teacher's aide. The other aides usually wore slacks. But Sue wore fancy dresses just so the principal would notice her.

_____ 6. Bill worked in a hardware store. He tried to keep up with the latest fads for his work clothes.

_____ 7. Calvin looked at himself in a full-length mirror every morning before he left for work to make sure he looked right for his job.

_____ 8. May wiped her purse down with a damp cloth to make sure it looked clean.

_____ 9. Frank hated to iron. So when he bought new clothes he looked at the label or asked the clerk if the item would need to be ironed.

Chapter 3

Getting Along with Your Boss

"One for all and all for one!" You, your boss, and your company are like the Three Musketeers: What's good for one is good for all!

Your boss is the most important person in your work life. The boss can make your job enjoyable or impossible. She or he can decide if you get a raise or promotion. She or he can play a large part in whether you feel good about your work and about yourself. In short, your boss can make or break you on the job. If you're smart, you'll get the boss on your side!

So, how can you do this? The first thing to do is make up your mind that you *will* get along with your boss. Even if the boss is not very friendly, it's up to you to get along with him or her if you want to KEEP THAT JOB!

> Derrick was a great mechanic. He had no trouble finding work. But he never seemed to last long on any one job. In fact, he had worked at 4 different jobs in the last year.
>
> Derrick said he'd just had bad luck with picky bosses. His first boss fired him for leaving tools lying around. The second boss fired him for arguing about some of the jobs he was asked to do. He lost the third job for talking about his boss behind her back. He lost his last job because he never finished his work on time.
>
> Derrick was a well-trained mechanic. But he was getting nowhere on the job. His problems had nothing to do with his work skills. Derrick needed a quick course in "Getting Along with Your Boss!"

Here are 11 great ways to get along with any boss:

28. Learn what's important to your boss.

Show her that these same things are important to you. For example, if neatness is a must with your boss, make sure your work and work area are neat.

29. Try to make your boss look good.

Do your job well and do whatever you can to make sure your workplace runs smoothly.

30. Accept jobs from your boss with a positive attitude.

Cooperate pleasantly in doing the jobs you're given. Help out by offering to do an unwanted task that needs doing.

31. Follow the boss's directions.

Be sure you understand what is expected of you. Listen carefully. If you're not sure, ask!

32. Learn to take criticism in stride.

No one likes to be corrected. But it is part of being a boss to let workers know if the job's not being done right. So, don't get angry. Instead, listen and try to learn from your mistakes.

33. Be loyal to your boss.

Don't talk about him behind his back. Your comments may be repeated and find their way back to the boss.

34. Be loyal to the company you work for.

Have a positive attitude toward the company and its goals. Loyal workers make a stronger company. And a stronger company is in a better position to do more for its workers.

35. Be willing to work!

Hard work is not always fun. But doing a job well *is* a good feeling. Trying to get away with the least amount of work doesn't make you or your boss feel good. Give a fair day's work for your pay.

36. Do your job the best you can.

Know what your job is and how it is to be done. Take pride in your work. Be sure it is done right and on time.

37. Be a worker the boss knows she can depend on.

Be on time to work, or a little early, each day. Finish work on time. Lateness is one of bosses' biggest gripes about workers.

38. Obey the rules of the company.

When you start a new job, find out what the rules are. Ask for help if you don't understand some of them. Then follow the rules even if you don't like some of them.

■ CAN YOU GET ALONG WITH THE BOSS? ■

Circle the best way to get along with each boss below.

1. Your boss is really fussy about cleaning up after each plumbing job. You should

    a. spend a few extra minutes cleaning up.

    b. try to get him to loosen up.

    c. get him to do that part of the job.

2. You think your boss may have forgotten about an important meeting. You should

    a. say nothing. It's not your problem.

    b. ~~remind her privately.~~

    c. tell everyone you remembered, but she forgot. She will be impressed with your memory.

3. The boss gives you a new job to do. You should

    a. explain why you don't have time to do it.

    b. groan loudly and complain about your work load to everyone who will listen.

    c. ~~accept the job pleasantly.~~

4. The boss gives you directions for how a job is to be done. You've tried to understand, but you really don't. You should

    a. ~~ask for more directions.~~

    b. pretend to understand so you don't look stupid.

    c. keep trying to figure it out on your own the best you can.

5. Your boss tells you he doesn't like the way you did a job. He wants it done over. You should

    a. immediately tell him why your way is better.

    b. get upset. Let him know how hard you worked.

    c. ~~stay calm. If you have a good reason, explain why you did it your way. If he still disagrees, do it over his way.~~

6. Your boss really messed up on a big job. You should

    a. make yourself look good by telling everyone you knew it would never work.

    b. tell everyone what a rotten boss she is.

    c. ~~keep quiet.~~

(continued)

7. You have an idea for a way to save your company money. You should

    a. keep quiet. Don't rock the boat.

    b. tell your co-workers how dumb the present way is.

    (c.) share your idea with the boss privately, even though you think he may use the idea and say it is his.

8. On your first job you're asked to do many simple, boring tasks. You should

    a. refuse to do them. You're above all that.

    (b.) do your best on each task you're given.

    c. try to get away with the least work possible.

9. You sew buttonholes in a clothing factory. It's the same thing over and over. You should

    (a.) take pride in doing each buttonhole neatly and correctly.

    b. do a quick job, even if it's not so neat.

    c. do as little work as possible.

10. Many of your co-workers are late to work, and they seem to get away with it. You should

    (a.) be on time anyway.

    b. come in as late as they do, but no later.

    c. tell the boss on them.

11. Some of the rules of your new company seem too strict. You should

    (a.) follow the rules even if you don't like them.

    b. follow only the rules you agree with.

    c. complain to all your co-workers.

■ WHO'S IN CONTROL? ■

Your boss controls many things about your work life. But you have some control, too. You can make your job more pleasant with a good attitude.

Listed below are some things that are part of doing a job. Tell how much control a worker has over each thing (a lot, some, none, etc.). Then tell why you feel as you do. There can be more than one right answer.

1. Being happy with your job

   — You don't need to like your job. All that is required of you is to get the work done. You should have full control over this.

2. Getting along with your boss

   — You should try to get along with your boss so it makes your job easier. It is your choice how well you get along with your boss.

3. Being accepted as part of a work team

   — Be happy and glad that you get along with your co-workers and it makes your job faster and easier. You will have some control over this.

4. Getting a raise or promotion

   — You have the most control whether or not you get a raise. You should be happy but don't brag about it to everyone.

5. Doing your job well

   — You will have control over how good a job you do, but it's all in your personal effort.

(continued)

6. Getting the boss "on your side"

    It's never a good idea to start playing teacher's pet otherwise your co-workers will turn on you.

7. Being given more responsibility

    Being given more responsibility is what you have some control over. That is when you need to start showing extra effort.

8. Getting known as a dependable person

    This is always the best feeling and you know you that others can depend on you to get the job done.

■ HANDLING CRITICISM ■

Being criticized by your boss is no fun. But it's part of any job.

If you make a mistake:

> Don't whine.
> Don't make excuses.
> Don't blame someone else.

Own up to your mistake. Say you're sorry. Try to do better next time!

Directions: Write a good answer to each boss's criticism.

1. *Boss:* You're not doing a good job keeping the coffee break area clean.	*You:* I'm sorry I'll try to do a better job next time.
2. *Boss:* You have been late with your work twice this week.	*You:* I will try to work faster and put more effort into my work.

(continued)

3. *Boss:* You are not following the company rules about lunch breaks. You may eat between 1:00 and 2:00 only.	*You:* I must have misunderstood. I will obey the company rules from now on.
4. *Boss:* You forgot three stops on your delivery route and the customers are angry!	*You:* I will look at map more next time and try to get to the customers quicker.
5. *Boss:* Your clothes are not right for this job. You must follow the company dress code.	*You:* I will do better next time. I will have the right clothes ready.

Chapter 4

Getting Along with Your Co-workers

Be a team player! Don't drop the ball when it's in your corner. Cooperate for the good of the team.

Being part of a group of workers is much easier if you all get along. If you "fit in" with your co-workers, you'll be more likely to KEEP THAT JOB!

To get along, you need many kinds of "people" skills. You must know how to be part of a team. You must know how to make friends. You must also know how to handle conflicts.

> Miguel worked on a construction crew. He was hardworking and made few mistakes. Miguel was always on time, hardly ever absent, and willing to work overtime. But when it was promotion time, Miguel was always passed over. He couldn't understand why.
>
> Even though Miguel's work habits were great, he couldn't get along with his co-workers. He was a loner and didn't even try to be friendly to anyone.
>
> Miguel put down others who worked slower or made mistakes. If someone had a plan he disliked, he argued loudly and "put the other person in his place." Miguel knew he was better at his job than any other worker, and he took every chance to point it out.
>
> Miguel had good work skills. But he would go further on the job if he could learn to *get along with his co-workers*.

Being Part of the Team

Here are 6 ways to get along with your co-workers:

39. Do your share of the work.

Be sure you're holding up your end. Get your part of the job done right and on time so the team looks good. Don't ask others to cover for you when you're late or do poor work.

40. Treat your co-workers with respect.

If you don't like someone, try to keep it to yourself. Don't gossip about your co-workers. Running down others just makes *you* look bad.

41. Listen to co-workers' ideas respectfully.

This is especially important if that person has been on the job longer than you have. That "old-timer" has learned a lot over the years that you may need to know too.

42. If you disagree with someone, do so in a calm, polite way.

You'll get more respect if you don't get angry.

43. Be a team player.

Cooperate to do what's best for the team and the company as a whole. Help out newer workers.

■ CAN YOU GET ALONG WITH YOUR CO-WORKERS? ■

Circle the letter of the best way to get along with your co-workers in each situation below.

1. You and three other workers share a job. They want to divide the work so each person does 1/4. The job is harder for you because you're new, so you don't think that's fair.

    ⓐ Buck up and really try to do your share of the work.

    b. Tell the others you want a smaller share of the work.

    c. Complain to your boss.

2. You don't like one of the people you have to work with.

    (a.) Be honest and say so.

    b. Keep it to yourself and try to be nice.

    c. Tell your boss you won't work with that person.

3. One of your co-workers is handicapped.

    a. Make jokes about it. The person should be used to it.

    (b.) Accept the person.

    c. Avoid the person.

4. An older member of your work team often tells you how things should be done. You'd rather do it your way.

    (a.) Listen to the advice. The person may know something you don't.

    b. Tell the person not to bother you.

    c. Ignore him. He's probably out of date anyway.

5. You disagree with a co-worker's plan for doing a job.

    (a.) Tell her why in a calm way, giving your reasons.

    b. Laugh at her.

    c. Argue loudly so everyone will see how smart you are.

6. A new worker joins your team.

    a. Let him find his own way. You had to.

    (b.) Help him out whenever you can.

    c. Ignore him until he proves himself.

■ *YES OR NO?* ■

Read each sentence below. Write **Yes** if the person followed the rules for getting along with co-workers. Write **No** if the person did not.

___No___ 1. George always asked one of his co-workers to finish his work for him when he needed to leave early.

__no__ 2. Sal took long lunch hours and asked a friend to cover for her.

__no__ 3. Mr. Blair had been a carpenter for 30 years. Mike figured Mr. Blair was too old to know what he was doing, so he didn't listen when Mr. Blair gave him advice.

__yes / no__ 4. Meg didn't like Roxie at all. She tried not to show it.

__no__ 5. Omar didn't like Van. He told everyone why, hoping that Van might get fired.

__yes__ 6. Lee didn't think Marty's plan for building a deck would work. He spoke up and politely told Marty his reasons.

■ How Do You Rate? ■

Put an X in the column that best tells how you rate in your ability to get along with others (at work or at school).

	Usually	Sometimes	Never
1. I do my share of the work.	X		
2. I treat others with respect.	X		
3. I avoid gossip.	X		
4. I disagree calmly and politely.	X		
5. I'm a friend to others.	X		
6. I avoid hurting others' feelings.	X		
7. I'm loyal to my friends.	X		

(continued)

8. I avoid bragging.	X			
9. I can work well with a team.	X			
10. I avoid borrowing money.	X			
11. I look on the bright side.	X			
12. I'm interested in others.	X			
13. I'm happy for others when they do well.	X			
14. I'm a team player.	X			

Friends at Work

Making friends with your co-workers can make your workday more fun. Here are 7 ways to make friends at work:

44. Be interested in your co-workers.

Learn their names. Listen when they talk. Let them know you like them. Be willing to help out a co-worker when she needs it.

45. Be considerate.

Try not to do things that will anger or hurt anyone. Treat people the way you like to be treated.

46. Be loyal to your co-workers.

Don't talk behind anyone's back. Friendships are built on trust. If you are two-faced, others won't trust you.

47. Don't brag about how good you are.

If you're good at a job, everybody can see that you are.

48. Don't make a habit of borrowing money from your co-workers.

If you do borrow, be sure to pay it back quickly.

49. Don't complain all the time.

Be happy! You'll be more fun to be around if you look on the bright side.

50. Praise your co-workers for their successes.

Cheer for your co-workers when they get a promotion, a bonus, or praise from the boss. They'll be on your team when you do well.

■ *What Would You Do?* ■

Tell what you would do in each of the following situations. Give your reasons.

1. You're new in the office. You hope you'll make friends at work.

   - try my best to meet people and make new friends.
   - Because there is always a chance to make new relationships.

2. A co-worker's husband is in the hospital. You want to help her out.

   - I would try to give her words of comfort and give her a get well card and try to make her feel happy again.

3. You are a smoker. You work in a room with 6 non-smokers. You don't want to bother anyone.

   - leave the room so I would not get second-hand smoke and just keep my personal or oppressive comments to myself.

4. A co-worker tells you a secret you know others would love to hear.

— I would just keep it to myself or just try to ignore him.

5. You're the fastest typist in the office. The other typists start talking about how fast they can type.

— I would avoid bragging and just ignore the others.

6. It's the end of the month. You're out of cash. A friend wants you to go out to lunch.

— I would tell him that we would have to take a rain check and apologize to him.

7. A co-worker gets in trouble with the boss.

— I would not stick around to listen and I would not make fun of him.

8. A co-worker gets the promotion you'd hoped to get.

— keep personal comments to myself and not make a big issue out of it.

Danger in the Workplace

> Carlos got a job in a dry cleaning plant. Carlos made friends easily. He was soon part of the team.
>
> The other workers liked to stop by and talk with Carlos as he worked. Lunches and coffee breaks always seemed to run long, as it was hard to stop visiting.
>
> Then Carlos began dating a girl who worked in the dry cleaning plant office. He saw her whenever he could think of an excuse to go up to the office.
>
> One day Carlos' boss called him in. He said he was afraid Carlos didn't have his mind on his work lately. If things didn't get better fast, he'd have to let Carlos go. Carlos was stunned! What had gone wrong?

We've just talked about making friends at work. It's good to be on friendly terms with your co-workers. But when you're at work, the job must come first if you want to KEEP THAT JOB! Remember these 4 hints:

51. Don't take too long for coffee breaks or lunch breaks.

Remember you're at work to do a job. Wasting a lot of time talking or taking long breaks will not make your boss happy.

52. Choose your friends carefully when you start a new job.

Get to know the other workers before you get too chummy with one group or person. You may find out too late that someone is on the "outs" with the boss. Or a new "friend" may not hold the same values you do.

53. Don't pick up bad habits in order to "fit in."

If a lot of your co-workers chew tobacco, for example, you don't need to start too. This won't make them like or dislike you.

54. Stay away from "complainers."

Avoid those who are always griping about the job or the boss. You don't want the boss to think of you as a complainer.

■ *Do You Agree?* ■

Tell if you agree with each statement below. Give your reasons.

1. Doing a great job is more important than being friends with your co-workers.

   I disagree with this, because in order to get a job done you have to learn to make friends.

2. Don't make friends at work. You're there to do a job.

I completely disagree with this statement as well. You are there to work but you can still make friends with your co-workers.

3. Other workers won't like you if you don't go out with them after work every night.

I disagree, it is completely your choice who you want to make friends with. What matters is that they like you for who you are.

4. Make friends as quickly as possible when you start a new job.

I disagree, sometimes it's better to take things slow and take time when you go around making friends.

5. Be a friend to others if you want to make friends.

I completely agree with this, if you want to make friends then by all means be friendly to others.

6. Gossiping about the boss is fine as long as he doesn't hear you.

- I disagree completely, it is never a good idea to gossip about other people or much less your employer behind their back.

7. Talking loudly will make others value your opinions more.

I disagree, you should never speak out and become a leader it shows how much you like bragging.

Chapter 5

Doing Your Best Work

"Whatever your life's work is, do it well. A man should do his job so well that the living, the dead and the unborn could do it no better.

If it falls your lot to be a street sweeper, sweep streets like Michelangelo painted pictures, like Shakespeare wrote poetry, like Beethoven composed music; sweep streets so well that all the hosts of heaven and earth will have to pause and say, 'Here lived a great street sweeper, who swept his job well.'"

—Martin Luther King, Jr.

Not everyone can be a straight A student. Or a star basketball player. Or president of a large company. But everyone can use his or her abilities to do the best job possible.

Scientists say most people use only 10 percent of their true ability. If that is true, we can all stretch a little further to use our abilities more fully.

Doing a job well gives you a sense of satisfaction and confidence. By doing less than your best, you fail yourself. There is no job unworthy of doing well. By using your talents, you'll expand them.

Here are 8 key work habits you'll need in order to do your best work:

55. Do more than is required of you.

Learn to do your job well. Study, listen, and try to learn as much about your job as you can.

56. Work until the job is done.

Don't give up if the going gets tough. Finish each job you're given.

57. Be reliable.

Be a person who can be counted on to get the job done—on time and correctly.

58. Be orderly.

Keep your work space neat and in order.

59. If you make a mistake, correct it quickly.

Use mistakes as a way to learn how to do your job better the next time.

60. Use your time well.

Make a list of what you need to do. Do the most important jobs first. Then work your way down the list. Avoid putting off work that has to be done.

61. Ask questions when you don't understand.

Asking a "dumb question" could stop you from *doing* something dumb.

> **62. Take pride in your work.**

Even if you don't like your job, do your best. By doing one job well, you may get a chance at a better job later. And, just as important, you'll feel pride in yourself for a job done well.

■ *YOUR WORK HABITS* ■

Think about your work habits. Put an X under the column that best tells about your work habits (at school or on the job).

	All the time	Most of the time	Sometimes	Never
1. If I say I'll be somewhere at a certain time, I'll be on time.	X			
2. If I get an assignment, I finish it on time.	X			
3. After doing a job, I clean up after myself.	X			
4. If given directions, I remember them and follow them.	X			
5. If I make a mistake, I try to correct it the next time.	X			
6. I'm willing to work as hard as needed to finish a job.	X			
7. I work well in a group.	X			
8. I finish every job.	X			
9. I work independently.	X			

(continued)

	All the time	Most of the time	Sometimes	Never
10. I try to learn as much as I can about every job	X			
11. I avoid wasting time.	X			
12. I ask questions if I don't understand something.	X			
13. I work neatly.	X			
14. I see things that need to be done and do them.	X			
15. I take pride in doing a better-than-average job.	X			

Do you have most of your marks in the "All the time" or "Most of the time" columns? ___All the time___

Looking at the items you marked "Sometimes" or "Never," which of your work habits could be better? ___none___

■ BE POSITIVE! ■

Why are the following negative attitudes harmful to the company and to yourself?

1. Doing the least work you can get away with
   ___It shows that you do not want to a productive worker.___

2. Thinking you are too good for a job and giving it the least effort possible
   ___It won't be sold or will end up not working properly___

3. Leaving a mess behind you

   makes you look irresponsible and that you can't clean up after yourself.

4. Not trying to learn more about your job

   shows you have no will to work and that you have no interest in your work

5. Putting off jobs you really don't want to do

   you might end up procrastinating which turns into a bad habit.

6. Being afraid to ask questions when you don't understand something

   indicates you don't want to learn or ask when you're not sure.

7. Being so upset when you make a mistake that you don't want to try again

   getting overly upset at making a little mistake will make you believe you can't do it.

8. Being late with assignments

   is the same as being late for work, if you are late with an assignment, then it shows you are not responsible.

9. Being ashamed of your job

   makes you regret going to work in the morning.

■ What Do You Think? ■

1. You start out with the lowest-ranked job in the company. What work habits do you think would be the most important to help you work your way up to a better job?

   - working hard
   - helping others
   - getting your jobs done

2. How can enjoying your job help you do a better job?

   - won't make the weeks or days seem so long

3. How could feeling sorry for yourself because of a handicap affect your success on the job?

   - decreases your work effort
   - slows you down
   - prevents you from working

4. Winston Churchill once said: "There are no small parts, only small actors." How does this statement apply to a place of work?

   - everyone helps to do the big jobs and those that don't, act up.

5. The best quarterbacks make only 6 out of 10 passes. What does this tell us about success on the job?

   - that out of lots of other employees only six out of those other 10 will get promoted.

6. How could blaming others for your mistakes stop you from doing well on the job?

- makes you waste valuable time
- slows you down
- starts an argument

7. *You* choose your attitude. How can a positive attitude help you on the job?

- helps you work harder
- helps you to complete your work
- makes the time spent working faster

Chapter 6

Communication Skills

Vic was new at his job in a fast food restaurant. Nadia was assigned to show him around the first day. Nadia introduced Vic to the other workers. Later she was surprised when he didn't remember any of their names. Vic answered that he was working to make money, not friends.

Daniel's boss, Mr. Valdez, came up to Daniel on the job site. He smiled and asked Daniel how things were going. Daniel answered him with a list of problems he was having at home. His boss listened, but quickly walked off.

Carmel worked in a children's clothing store. Often customers called wanting to know if the store carried a certain brand or color of clothing. Carmel thought answering these questions over the phone just wasted her time. After all, she thought, the person phoning may not even come in. So Carmel handled these calls in a short, rapid-fire manner. One day a customer came in and complained to the manager that Carmel was rude to her on the phone.

What do Vic, Daniel, and Carmel have in common? All three are headed for problems: either with the boss, co-workers, or customers. All three need to work on their communication skills.

Most unhappiness at work is caused by "people problems." One way to avoid these problems is to learn good communication skills.

Communication has two parts: speaking and listening. First we'll take a look at good speaking skills.

Speaking Skills

Here are 9 ways to speak so others will listen:

> **63. Speak clearly and speak so others can hear you.**

Don't yell. Don't mumble.

> **64. Avoid using slang and don't swear at work.**

Some people are offended by such talk (maybe your boss).

> **65. Don't interrupt when someone else is talking.**

> **66. If someone compliments you, smile and say "thank you."**

> **67. Don't try to cover up your mistakes.**

If you owe someone an apology, go to her right away and admit your mistake.

68. Say "no" if asked to do something you think is wrong.

Don't be afraid to stand up for your rights.

69. Learn to disagree with others in a pleasant way.

Don't yell, call the other person names, or make fun of his ideas.

70. Don't whine and complain.

Everybody has troubles; they don't want to hear about yours all the time.

71. Make the other person glad she talked to you.

Give compliments. Talk about something she is interested in. Your positive attitude will spread to others around you. But be genuine. Don't overdo it.

Listening Skills

The second half of communication is listening. Listening is more than just not talking. And listening is more *important* than talking—and often more difficult to do.

Being a good listener can bring you friends and more success on the job. Here are 5 ways to become a good listener.

72. Listen carefully when you're introduced to someone.

Ask if you don't hear the name. Try to remember people's names. Repeat the person's name when you're introduced: "Nice to meet you, Jack." Remembering people's names makes them feel good.

73. Listen when you're given directions.

Take notes if you need to in order to remember.

74. Listen to learn what's going on around you at work.

You can learn more about your job and the company you work for.

75. Give the person speaking to you your full attention.

Make eye contact. Act interested. Ask questions. This makes the other person feel important.

76. Make sure you understand what the other person is saying.

To be sure you understand, repeat the main idea in your own words.

■ *What Do You Think?* ■

1. Not listening to others can cost *everyone.* What do you think might happen if . . .

    a. a boss won't listen to her workers?

    - The workers won't know what to do
    - the workers won't solve his/her problem
    - the workers will have a hard time focusing

    b. a salesperson doesn't listen to the customers?

    - the store won't make a sale
    - the customer will be mad

    c. a worker doesn't listen to his co-workers?

    - the workers won't get along
    - they won't get their work done
    - they will be wasting time

2. Why do you think listening has been called the "greater half" of communication?

- because information gets across
- problems get solved

■ Do You Agree? ■

Read each statement below. Tell why you agree or disagree with the statement.

1. If you maintain eye contact with the person you're speaking to, he'll feel like you're staring at him.

I disagree, because if you keep eye contact with who you are talking to it shows you are listening.

2. It's O.K. to interrupt someone only if what you have to say is more important.

I agree because if what you really have to say IS important than you can interrupt, but if it's not then you shouldn't interrupt.

3. When you get a compliment, shrug it off.

I disagree, if someone compliments you you should feel happy and accept it.

4. If you owe someone an apology, forget about it. He or she will soon forget, too.

5. You should do everything the boss asks you to, even if it's against your beliefs.

   I disagree. You really shouldn't do anything that you feel you shouldn't do.

6. Swearing a lot makes you look more mature.

   I disagree. Swearing does not make you look more mature it just makes you look bad and makes people look down on you.

7. If you don't understand someone's name when you are introduced, pretend you did.

   I disagree about this because if you are introduced to someone you should try to remember that person's name.

8. Taking notes when you are given directions makes you look dumb.

   I disagree, if you are taking notes while given directions shows you are listening.

9. Mind your own business at work. Don't try to learn about the company. Just learn your own job.

   I disagree you should try to learn as much as you can about the company as you can.

10. If you gossip a lot, you'll be a more interesting person to listen to.

    I disagree if you gossip alot it will make people dislike you more.

Using the Telephone at Work

Pretend you are a customer of the Handy Hardware Store. What would you think if you called the store to see if they carry cordless drills and . . .

- the clerk puts you on hold and forgets about you?
- the clerk answers your questions in a short, hurried manner?
- the clerk takes a message for one of the salespeople to call you back, but he never does?
- no one answers the phone?
- the clerk tells you to come in and look around yourself for the item you want?
- the clerk is unfriendly?

How would you feel if you were treated poorly on the telephone? Would you go to Handy Hardware to shop? Or, would you shop somewhere else?

The telephone is a business link with the outside world. It is an important part of a business's success. If answering the phone is part of your job, do the best you can at it. Here are 7 ways to make your company look good:

77. Answer business phone calls on the first or second ring.

This makes your company look well run.

78. Answer the phone in a friendly, helpful manner.

If you are rude or in a hurry, the customer may go somewhere else to shop. Good phone manners will impress your boss and all those who call.

79. Know how your boss wants you to answer the phone.

(Your boss probably has something in mind.) You should state the name of the company, identify yourself, and then ask if you can be of help. "Elroy's Auto Parts. This is Biff speaking. May I help you?", for example.

80. Make sure you get the caller's name right.

If you need to ask the caller's name, say "Who is calling, please?" When the caller gives his name, repeat it. Address the caller by Mr. or Ms., unless you are told to do otherwise.

81. Learn to take good, complete phone messages.

If you need to ask take a message, be sure to get: (a) the name of the caller, (b) the caller's phone number, (c) the message, and (d) the time and date of the call.

After you get the message, repeat it to the caller to make sure it is right.

82. Don't keep people waiting too long "on hold."

First, offer to take a message instead. If you do put a caller on hold, check back with her often so she knows you haven't forgotten about her.

83. Keep a pleasant attitude on the phone.

Don't let a rude caller make you lose your cool. If you stay pleasant and helpful, the caller may calm down. At any rate, it makes your company look bad if you get angry or rude on the phone.

■ *PROBLEM CALLERS* ■

Read each situation below. Write what you would say to each caller.

1. A caller demands to talk to your boss. You answer that your boss is in a meeting and cannot be disturbed. The caller gets angry and swears at you. What do you do?

   _____

   _____

   _____

2. You work in the library. A caller wants to know if the book *Call it Courage* has been checked out. You don't have time to go look because a long line of people are waiting to check out books. What do you do?

   _____

   _____

   _____

3. You work for a dentist. A caller wants to make an appointment to see the dentist. He is a new patient. You have been told to get the name, address, and phone number of each new patient before

you give them a time to come in. The caller refuses to give you this information. What do you do?

_____

_____

_____

4. You work in the billing department at a store. A caller complains that her bill is too high. You look at the records and see that she charged $219 last month. She says she doesn't remember charging anything. What do you do?

_____

_____

_____

5. You work for a building company. A caller has some questions about a job your company is doing at his home. You answer him correctly and politely. Later your boss tells you that the customer complained about your poor grammar and sloppy speech. What do you do?

_____

_____

_____

Dealing with Customers

> Todd and Lou sold shoes. Todd often waited on several customers at one time. He never "wasted time" talking to customers or being very friendly.
>
> Lou, on the other hand, looked at his customers differently. He was friendly and helpful. He tried to give his customers personal attention and make them glad they'd come in.
>
> Both Todd and Lou worked on *commission*. The more shoes they sold, the more money they made. Every month Lou outsold Todd. His customers kept coming back, and they kept buying shoes.

Lou had learned that taking good care of his customers really paid off! Good customers are hard to find and even harder to keep. If you work in sales and want to KEEP THAT JOB, you must learn to deal with your customers well.

Be helpful and be friendly. Customers are likely to return if you give good service and make them happy they came in. You could look at it this way: Both the salesperson and the boss in a business are really working for the customer. That's because without the customer there would be no business. Here are 6 ways to do a good job handling customers:

84. Greet each customer with a friendly smile.

If you can't wait on a new customer right away, let him know you will be with him as soon as possible.

85. If you're in sales, know your product or service well.

Be able to answer any questions the customer may have. If you don't know the answer to a question, ask someone who does. Have a positive attitude about the product or service your company offers.

86. Treat customers as you would like to be treated.

Be honest. Be polite. Make the customer feel important.

87. Don't ignore customers or keep them waiting too long.

People will usually be patient if they see you are busy. Let them know you'll get to them as soon as you can.

88. Handle customer complaints pleasantly.

Listen carefully to the complaint and be sure you understand. Don't argue with the customer. Follow the rules of the business in handling the complaint. Offer a refund, a replacement, etc., and do so cheerfully. If you are not sure how to handle the situation, get the help of a manager.

89. Always thank the customer for coming in.

■ *Do You Agree?* ■

Tell if you agree or disagree with each statement. Then give your reasons.

1. If you are talking with a customer on the phone, you should not keep a customer in the store waiting for more than a minute or two.

   _____

   _____

2. If you talk down to a customer, the customer will be impressed with how smart you are.

   _____

   _____

3. If you dress in a businesslike way, the customer will have more confidence in what you say.

   _____

   _____

4. If a customer has a complaint about your product, argue at length about why he is wrong.

   _____

   _____

5. If a product is damaged, sell it anyway. After all, it's up to the buyer to beware.

   _____

   _____

6. Make the customer feel important and you'll get more sales.

   _____

   _____

7. The customer is always right!

   _____

   _____

Chapter 7

Problems at Work

Stress at Work

Brent's boss was always on his case. It seemed Brent could do nothing right. The boss yelled at him all day long. When Brent got home, he yelled at his wife and kids.

Lucy worked at the service desk in a store. All day long she answered the phone and handled customer complaints, usually both at the same time. By the end of the day, she was too tired to do anything except get fast food to eat in front of the TV.

Mitch's boss, on the other hand, thought he was great. He knew he could count on Mitch to do a good job. So he piled on one job after another. Mitch was always worried about how he could get everything done.

Brent, Lucy, and Mitch all have a lot of stress in their jobs. Many workers do. They may have too much to do, like Lucy and Mitch. They may have a difficult boss as Brent does. Short of changing jobs, how can you learn to cope with stress? Here are 7 ways to handle stress on the job:

90. Exercise can help reduce stress.

Even a brisk 20-minute walk 3 times a week can do wonders for reducing stress and keeping you fit.

91. A balanced diet helps you stand up to stress.

Don't skip meals. If your body is getting the nutrients it needs, you'll be better able to handle stress.

92. Enough sleep gives you energy to face the day.

Being tired can make you edgy and unable to do your best work.

93. Don't worry about things you can't control.

Everything at work may not be just as you'd like it to be. But try to learn not to let things bother you.

94. Do the most important jobs first.

Decide which things are the most important and make sure they get done first. Then you'll be less upset about other small jobs that you can't finish.

95. Take time in your life to do something you enjoy.

It could be a sport or hobby. It could be helping others. Anything that lets you focus on something other than your problems will help.

96. Learn ways to relax.

Meditation, prayer, or relaxation exercises can help. Talking over problems with a friend or family member can make you feel better. Learn what works for you.

Discrimination

Anna and Louise worked in a doctor's office. Louise was 20 years older than Anna. Louise noticed that Anna always got the more interesting jobs to do. Louise was stuck with simple jobs that kept her tied to a desk all day. She was a victim of *age discrimination.*

Lila and Julia were hired at the same time as helpers in a large beauty shop. Lila was white; Julia was black. It became clear right away that Julia was getting the worst jobs and the worst working hours. Lila's jobs were easier and more fun. And she also got better working hours. Julia was a victim of *racial discrimination.*

Steve was a teller in a bank. He used a wheelchair. The bank manager put him at the last window where few customers would see him. He was given a lot of boring paperwork to do, which did not allow him to use his training to the fullest. Steve was a victim of *discrimination toward the handicapped.*

JoAnn and Ryan had both worked at the same job for the same length of time. One day JoAnn found out that Ryan was making $2 more per hour. JoAnn was a victim of *sexual discrimination.*

What do Louise, Julia, Steve, and JoAnn all have in common? All four were being discriminated against. Julia was treated unfairly because of her race. Louise was treated poorly because of her age. Steve was pushed aside because of his handicap. And JoAnn was discriminated against because of her sex.

Discrimination is unfair treatment of a person due to race, sex, age, religion, handicap, and so on. The Civil Rights Act of 1964 states that employers may not discriminate in hiring, firing, layoffs, wages, promotions, or training. To enforce the Civil Rights Act, the Equal Employment Opportunity Commission (EEOC) was set up.

Discrimination is against the law. But people's attitudes cannot always be controlled by laws. So you may meet discrimination when you take a job. If you do, there are several things you can do about it:

97. You may choose to ignore *minor* remarks or slights.

But you should never let others degrade you or make you feel ashamed.

98. Don't fight back on the same level.

If you need to defend yourself, try to avoid acting as badly as the person who started the trouble. This may cause the situation to get worse. Or you may get yourself in trouble. Try to handle the problem in a more mature manner.

99. Win the respect of others by doing your best work.

Prove that you are a valuable worker.

100. Get help to solve the problem if it is serious.

First, tell your boss. Your boss should be able to stop the problem. If that doesn't work, or if your boss is the cause of the discrimination, talk to your personnel department. Your union could be another source of help. If none of these things work, contact the EEOC or a lawyer.

Sexual Harassment

> The men in the factory where Carlotta worked loved telling dirty jokes during breaks. They didn't stop when she entered the room. Sometimes they joked about her, too.
>
> Margaret's boss told her that she would get a big raise if she stayed in his room on their business trip.
>
> Harry had a woman boss who couldn't keep her hands off him. Harry wasn't interested in her and wished she would leave him alone.

Carlotta, Margaret, and Harry were all victims of *sexual harassment.* Sexual harassment can take different forms. Carlotta was being harassed with words. Margaret was promised money for sex. Harry's boss was touching him in ways he didn't like.

What is sexual harassment? It is any sexual behavior that is ***unwanted and unwelcome.***

Sexual harassment can be verbal or physical. It makes the victim feel uncomfortable or ashamed. It often gets in the way of the victim's ability to do his or her job.

If sexual harassment happens to you, here are 6 ways to deal with it:

101. Don't ignore it.

No one should have to put up with sexual harassment!

102. Keep a written report of exactly what happened.

Write down dates, times, and witnesses, if any. Keep this information in a safe place (not in your desk at work). You will need this information if you need to file a complaint.

103. Tell the person harassing you to stop.

Just telling the person to stop often works. Or you could write the person a letter. List the times he has harassed you and tell him to stop. Keep a copy of the letter in a safe place.

104. If the harassment does not stop at once, tell your boss.

If your boss is the harasser, you will need to go to higher management.

105. If the problem continues without help from higher management, you can contact the Equal Employment Opportunity Commission (EEOC).

Look in the phone book under "U.S. Government."

106. The ACLU (American Civil Liberties Union) or a lawyer can also help you.

If you work for a small company, you may need to talk to the ACLU or a lawyer to get help.

Sexual harassment happens a lot on the job. Nearly half of women and 15 percent of men in the workplace say they've been sexually harassed. Remember, sexual harassment is against the law. You have a right to do your job in safety and dignity!

Romance in the Office

David and Lelia worked in the same company. They had fallen in love at work.

David and Lelia were together at lunch and on breaks. They held hands and snuck a few kisses. They avoided other workers. Soon, no one wanted to work on a project with either of them. David and Lelia had upset the whole work team.

Tony worked in the shipping department of a large firm. One day he met Darcie, who worked in the billing department.

From then on, Tony kept showing up in Darcie's department. He stood by her desk and talked to her. Darcie tried to tell him not to bother her while she was working. One day Tony overheard two other billing clerks joking about how Tony was making a fool of himself. Tony felt silly.

Dating people at work can be O.K. But it can become a problem too. David and Lelia were avoiding everyone else and making people uncomfortable with their open displays. Tony was getting in the way of Darcie doing her work. This caused hard feelings with the other workers.

If you are dating a co-worker, remember this:

107. Save the romance for after work.

You were hired to do a job. If you're spending too much time talking to or thinking about the other person, your work will suffer. You need to act businesslike on the job. Save the romance for after work.

108. Remember that at work the job must come first.

It's probably best not to date someone you work with closely. But if you do, the job must come first if you want to KEEP THAT JOB!

The Office Party

It was time for the yearly office party. This year it was to be held at the boss's home. All the workers were invited. Jean wanted to be sure the boss noticed her. She wore a low-cut dress that really showed off her figure. Her boss *did* notice, and so did his wife! Allen couldn't pass up the free drinks. He drank so much he could hardly stand up. The next day he had to call in sick. The boss didn't say anything, but he wasn't impressed. Russ was shy. He stayed in a corner talking to his best friend during the whole party. He did not greet any of the other guests or talk to the boss or his wife. The boss wondered why Russ was so unfriendly.

These 3 workers made the same mistake. They did not know that an office party is different from a party with your friends. At an office party you need to think "office," not "party."

You can have a good time at an office party, but not *too* good. If you overeat, get drunk, or let the flirting get out of hand, you'll be the talk of the office Monday morning.

If you're invited to an office party, keep these 6 tips in mind for making a good impression:

109. Accept the party invitation if at all possible.

Think of it as part of your job. You really are expected to attend.

110. Go easy on the drinks and don't take drugs.

If you drink alcohol, set yourself a limit of 1 or 2 drinks. Don't take any drugs, no matter who is offering.

111. Avoid sexy or unusual clothing. And dress nicely.

The rules for dressing right for the job apply to an office party as well.

112. Be sure to greet the boss and her family.

Be friendly. Introduce yourself to people you don't know.

113. Avoid telling jokes that may offend others. And don't be too loud.

The person you offend may be your boss!

114. Thank your boss for a great time before you leave.

Crime in the Workplace

> Maury was going home for the day. As he left he put a couple of boxes of nails and screws in his lunch box. He picked up a pipe wrench and hid it under his jacket.
>
> Lara put a box of envelopes, an electric pencil sharpener, and some expensive pens in her purse before she left work.
>
> Lou rang up items she wanted from the drugstore where she worked. She charged herself far less than the correct price.
>
> Lorenzo brought small amounts of drugs to work every day. He sold them to other workers on his breaks.
>
> Tam tried on clothes in the dressing room of the store where he worked. If he liked something, he put his own clothes back on over the store item.

All of these workers did things that weren't honest. Are these acts wrong? What would you do if you knew of someone doing things like this? It is hard to know what to do. There are no easy answers. But here are 3 things to think about:

115. If you see a minor wrongdoing, you might let it go.

No one wants to "squeal" on a co-worker. In some minor cases (like a co-worker taking home a company pen) you're probably better off to let it go.

116. You might choose to speak to the person alone.

You could ask the person if he has thought about what could happen if he got caught. Remind him that if you saw him, others might see him too.

117. In serious cases, you need to tell the boss.

Stealing company property or selling drugs are both crimes and should be reported.

Quitting Your Job

Most people don't work at just one job forever. You are likely to make several job changes during your working life.

If you are thinking of leaving your present job, take some time and think some more. Remember, no job is perfect. No job is free from problems. When you change jobs, you are trading the set of problems you have now for a new set. Think it through. Are those pastures really greener at the next job?

Wrong Reasons for Quitting a Job

118. Don't quit a good job just for a small pay raise.

Ida quit her job because she read an ad telling about a job paying fifty cents more per hour. She did get the new job, but she was very unhappy with the work she had to do. The extra money was not worth it.

119. Don't always compare your job with others.

If you're happy with your job, why worry about what someone else is doing? Roy liked his job. But his brother told him that his job was a lot more exciting. So Roy quit his job to take one like his brother's. Soon he was wishing for his old job back.

120. Don't change jobs in too much of a hurry.

Wait until you find something that you really want. Faith was bored with her job. She felt that *anything* was better than staying with it. She took the first job that came along. She soon found it was no better.

121. Don't quit in a huff based on one argument or problem.

Duke had an argument with his boss. He usually liked his job, but at that moment he was really angry. He wanted to quit and walk out. Duke needed to take time to cool off and think things through.

Good Reasons for Quitting a Job

We've talked about some wrong reasons for quitting a job. Now let's look at some reasons that make sense.

122. Look for another job if you can't do the work.

If you are not succeeding with the work after giving it a fair shot, you might want to try something else. Zoe was not doing well in her job as a child care worker. She had tried hard for nearly a year. Now she hated coming to work each day.

123. Look around for another job if you're bored stiff.

If your job is boring, you might want a change. Even though he was successful in his work, Barry was bored. He had totally lost interest in his job. Barry wanted more variety and challenge.

124. Look around if you can't advance on your job.

Pearl was working as a clerk in a family-owned business. Only family members were promoted, so she knew she'd be a clerk forever. She wanted a job where she could move up.

125. Look around if you and your company are a "bad fit."

Nell worked in a law firm. She was uncomfortable with what she saw as dishonesty on the part of some people working there.

If You Decide to Quit, Exit with Class!

We've talked about wrong and right reasons for leaving a job. If you're not happy with your job, carefully weigh the facts. If you decide a change in jobs is best, do it right. Here are 8 ways to exit with class:

126. If you quit, keep your old job until you have another.

This way you can take your time finding work that is right for you. You also want to keep that paycheck coming in. Money worries can add to the stress of looking for a job.

127. Keep doing your best work until you leave your old job.

If you start doing poor work, you may not be able to get a good recommendation from your boss when you do leave.

128. Leave behind a good image of yourself.

Just because you're leaving, don't start complaining about everything you've always hated about the company. Those negative words may come back to you. Maybe someday you'll want to rejoin the company. Or you may need a good reference from the company. Don't burn your bridges.

129. Tell your boss you're leaving before you tell co-workers.

You don't want your boss to find out your plans from the office gossip.

130. Give 2 weeks to 1 month notice.

This gives your boss a chance to find someone to take your place.

131. Do what you can to help your replacement.

Offer to show the new person the ropes before you leave.

Getting Fired or Laid Off

If you've read and tried to follow the 150 ways to *Keep Your Job*, you may never need this information. But read it anyway!

Sometimes good workers do get fired or laid off. A company may need to cut back. Business may be bad. Then the company may need to let good workers go.

If you do get fired or laid off, here are 9 ways to put your life back together:

132. Exit with class.

Even though you are shocked, hurt, or angry, leave a good impression of yourself by acting in a mature manner. Don't get angry or yell. This will make it clear that it *was* a good decision to fire you.

133. If you get fired, you were *fired,* you did not *quit.*

The difference is *very important*. If you quit a job by choice, you may not be able to get vacation pay, severance pay, or unemployment compensation.

134. You should get some severance pay.

The amount will depend on how long you've worked for the company, the level of your job, and the reason you were let go.

135. You should get paid for unused vacation time.

But it's up to you to ask for it.

136. Try to find out why you were fired.

If you think you were fired because of your work habits or your attitude, try to find out where you went wrong. Then you can try to learn from your mistakes.

137. Find out if you can keep your health insurance for a while.

In many larger companies, you may be able to keep your insurance coverage for a while, usually by paying for it yourself.

138. Ask for a letter of recommendation if there hasn't been a problem with your work or conduct.

139. Sign up for unemployment compensation.

Talk to your local unemployment office to find out what you need to do.

140. Start looking for a new job quickly.

Be sure you have a good answer to the question "Why did you leave your last job?" Your answer should be positive and should not put down your former boss or company.

■ WHAT DO YOU THINK? ■

If you agree with what each of the following people did, write **YES** on the line. If you disagree, write **NO**. Give a reason for your answer. (There may be more than one right answer.)

___No___ 1. Dana's boss gave her a quick hug for a job well done. Dana yelled at him to keep away from her.

it's too much personal contact; maybe ask him not to hug her.

___yes___ 2. Edwin made it a point to spend time talking with his boss and her husband at the office party.

___No___ 3. Lacy's boss always called the female secretaries "girls." Even though it made Lacy mad, she let it go.

You don't know how the secretaries will react. It's also insulting and patronizing

___no___ 4. Ford's job was driving him crazy. He never seemed to be able to get everything done. So he started skipping lunch every day in order to have more time to work.

he hurt physically or it will hurt his health.

___yes___ 5. Isabel and Paul worked in the same factory. They began dating, and it became serious. But at work they kept their feelings under wraps.

___no___ 6. Mario worked in a butcher shop. He took home meat for dinner every night without paying for it. He figured it was O.K. since he was only making minimum wage.

it's the same as stealing from the company.

___no___ 7. Hanna heard about a job like hers that paid fifty cents more per hour. She quit her job that day and went to apply for the other job.

you shouldn't quit your job just because it pays more.

___yes___ 8. Ferdo was fired for doing poor work. He asked the boss to sit down with him and tell him exactly where he went wrong.

always talk with your boss if he/she feels you did something wrong.

■ WHAT WOULD YOU DO? ■

Tell what you would do in each situation below. There may be more than one right answer.

1. Your boss makes sexy remarks to you. But he never touches you. What could you say to your boss to get the remarks to stop?

   To tell him to stop and you don't like it.

2. The office party is coming up. It will be at the boss's house. You really don't want to go. What should you do?

   Call the boss the night before and tell him that you made other plans.

3. You're by far the youngest worker in your office. You feel the others have no confidence in you because of your age. You decide this is age discrimination. What could you do to gain the confidence of the others?

— Show them how hard you can work and how much you're able to take on.

4. Your new job is very stressful. You find you can't relax even when you get home. What would you do?

— take deep breaths or try to meditate — take a hot bath

5. You are dating a co-worker. Your relationship is becoming serious. Others in the office notice and begin teasing. What would you do?

— try to ignore them or just learn to accept it.

6. You are a cashier at a grocery store. You notice a co-worker taking home groceries without paying for them. What would you do?

— Tell one of the bagging people to run after them and tell them that they didn't pay.

7. You have a fight with your boss. You feel like quitting your job then and there. What would you do?

— Sit down and have a one to one chat with your boss and discuss the problem.

8. You get fired. Your boss does not offer you any severance pay, unused vacation pay, or other benefits. You wonder if you should ask him.

— Sit down and ask him if you still receive benefits after being fired.

■ What Does It Mean? ■

Explain each statement below.

1. When it comes to office parties, think "office," not "party."

   don't go wild or crazy when at an office party, be proffessional

2. Discrimination is against the law, but people's attitudes can't be controlled by laws.

   Even though it is against the law, people have a choice about how to act towards other people.

3. Exercise, a balanced diet, and enough rest can help a person deal with job stress.

   These things are all a part of dealing with stress in the workplace.

4. If you date someone you work with, remember that when you're at work the job must come first.

   you shouldn't be in a relationship at work and try to keep things proffessional.

5. When you change jobs, you are trading your current set of problems for a new set.

   When you dislike your first job, and you transfer to another job you take those problems with you.

6. If you are fired, don't burn your bridges. Exit with class!

   don't blow it out of proportion when you get fired, keep your anger and emotions in tact until you're out the door.

Chapter 8

Getting Promotions and Raises

Getting a Promotion

Every promotion is two-thirds motion. Raises aren't given for coming to work every day and continuing to draw breath.

You've got to make it happen. Moving ahead on the job doesn't happen by accident. Unless you want to keep the same job forever, you need a plan.

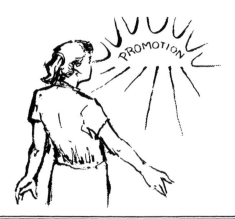

Terry had worked for the same company in the same job for 2 years. Her job was getting dull, and she was barely making enough money to make ends meet. Terry's boss showed no signs of offering her a promotion or a raise. Terry decided she'd better take action herself. First she thought about her work habits. She knew she had done her best work. She had been dependable. And she had studied hard to learn the ins and outs of her job. She'd studied the company and its products. Terry decided her work habits and attitude were not the reason she hadn't had a raise or promotion.

Next, Terry made a list of the reasons she should get a raise. She knew that when she talked to her boss about the raise, she'd be nervous. So she planned what she wanted to say ahead of time.

Terry was ready to talk to her boss now. She made an appointment at a time that was good for the boss. She told her boss why she felt she should get a raise. She told the boss she was also ready for more responsibility in her job.

Terry's boss listened quietly. He told Terry he'd need to talk it over with his boss and that he'd let her know. Terry thanked her boss for his time and left. For the next week Terry was on pins and needles. She knew better than to bug her boss. But it sure was hard waiting!

Finally Terry's boss called her in. He offered her a small raise. And he also put her in charge of an interesting project.

By thinking things through and making a plan, Terry had met both her goals.

Here are some good ways to get ahead on the job:

141. Learn more about your company.

Learn all you can about your own job and other jobs. Sign up for special training or schooling that is offered. Take adult education courses that interest you.

142. Do your very best at the job you have now.

Never complain or put down your job. As you become better at your job, you may get more responsibility. Remember the old saying, "There are no small parts, only small actors."

143. Check your work habits and attitude.

Be sure your work habits are what they should be. Keep your attitude positive. Be someone your boss can always count on to get the job done.

144. Set goals for yourself.

Make sure your goals are ones you hope to reach. Then work toward your goals.

145. Make yourself *look* like a successful person.

Many people get ahead because they make themselves *look* successful. They always look busy, never lazy. They look like they're working hard and doing a good job. And they also dress right for work.

■ *Right or Wrong?* ■

Write **right** by each statement that tells a good way to work toward a promotion. Write **wrong** by each statement that does not.

right 1. Have a positive attitude.

right 2. Do your best work at the job you now have.

Wrong 3. Let your boss know why your present job is really beneath someone with your abilities.

right 4. Take an adult education class.

Wrong 5. Complain how boring your job is.

Wrong 6. Don't bother with company training workshops unless you are forced to.

Wrong 7. Don't concern yourself with the company as a whole. It's not your business. Just worry about your own job.

right 8. Have goals you are working toward.

right 9. Be someone your boss can always depend on to get the job done.

right 10. Be positive about your job and your company.

right 11. Learn as much as you can about your company and its product or service.

right 12. Attend training courses offered by the company.

right 13. Learn all you can about your job.

Wrong 14. Do a good job and hope for the best. You don't really need a plan to get ahead.

Wrong 15. Make fun of your present job. Your boss will admire the way you think things through.

■ WILL YOU GET AHEAD ON THE JOB? ■

Rate yourself on each statement by putting an X in the correct box. (If you don't have a job now, think of your teacher as your boss and your classmates as co-workers.)

	Usually	Some of the time	Rarely
1. I am clean and well groomed.	X		
2. I dress neatly and suitably.	X		
3. I get along well with my boss.	X		
4. I work well with my co-workers.	X		
5. I cooperate with my boss.	X		
6. I do my best work.	X		
7. I'm on time to work.	X		
8. I use my time at work well.	X		
9. I keep learning about my job.	X		
10. I get the job done.	X		
11. I work well without supervision.	X		
12. I try to improve at my job.	X		
13. I willingly take on new jobs.	X		
14. I never neglect my jobs, even if they're boring to me.	X		

(continued)

	Usually	Some of the Time	Rarely
15. I follow the rules.	X		
16. I take responsibility for my mistakes; I try to learn from them.	X		
17. I take any extra on-the-job training courses that are offered.	X		
18. I am considerate of others.	X		
19. I work to develop my speaking and listening abilities.	X		
20. I follow the tips given in *150 Ways to Keep Your Job*.	X		

How to Get a Raise

You may be lucky and get a raise without asking for it. But then again, you may not!

If you've done a good job for a year or so, you may think it's time for a raise. Plan your approach carefully. Here are some things to think about before you ask for that raise:

146. List the reasons you think you should get a raise.

Include extra work you've done, extra schooling you've finished since taking the job, and new responsibilities you've taken on. Don't expect to get more money just for showing up every day.

147. Talk to your boss when you think he'll be in a good mood.

Make an appointment to talk at a time that's good for your boss. It's a good idea to pick a time when things are going well in the company or in your department.

148. Keep your talk positive and businesslike.

Don't whine about how little money you're making. Don't get angry or threaten to quit if you don't get more money. (The boss may take you up on it!)

149. Give your boss time to think it over.

You may not get your raise at once. Or she may have to discuss it with "higher-ups." If so, be patient. If you've heard nothing after 2 weeks, ask if a decision has been made. Be pleasant and don't make a pest out of yourself by asking too often.

150. If you're turned down, try to find out why.

Maybe you need to improve your attitude, work habits, or grooming. Or maybe it's just bad timing for the company. Finding out the reason will give you a better chance of a raise later.

Remember, some companies are not always fair about giving raises. Just because you deserve a raise doesn't mean you will always get one. You might also find out that a co-worker who has been with the company less time than you has been given a raise. Or someone who always seems to be goofing off was given one. If you have done your best work and get no raise after you've asked, you might want to look for another job.

■ WILL THIS PERSON GET A RAISE? ■

Each person below wanted a raise or promotion. Write **YES** if you think the person did the right thing. Write **NO** if you think they did not. Give reasons for your answers.

yes 1. Carly kept a list in her desk. She wrote down all the extra projects she did for the company. She gave the list to her boss when she asked for a raise.

_no_ 2. Earl wanted to ask for a raise. He decided his boss wouldn't be busy first thing Monday morning. He went in to see his boss at 7:30 a.m.

_no_ 3. Paula pointed out to her boss how much everything costs these days. She tried to make her boss feel sorry for her.

_no_ 4. Jimmy asked for a raise. His boss said he'd have to think about it. Two weeks later, Jimmy still hadn't heard. So he asked his boss how the raise was coming.

_no_ 5. Joel asked for a raise and was turned down. He wanted to know the reason, but he was afraid to ask.

_no_ 6. Cora asked her boss for a raise. She listed the extra courses and workshops she'd taken. She reminded her boss that she had many more responsibilities now than when she was hired.

_no_ 7. Melinda told her boss she'd have to quit if she couldn't come up with a raise.

_no_ 8. Aaron had been at work every day since he started 3 months ago. He told his boss he was due a raise for being so dependable.

_____no_____ 9. Even though times were hard at the company and several workers had been laid off, Liz asked her boss for a raise.

_____no_____ 10. Julie's boss told her he'd need more time to think about giving her a raise. She asked him about it every day to make sure he didn't forget.

Summary

150 Ways to Keep Your Job

The First Day on the Job

1. Get to work on time.
2. Ask your boss what he or she would like to be called.
3. Introduce yourself to your co-workers.
4. Show that you are willing to learn.
5. Go all out to do your best work.
6. Find out the *unwritten rules* of your workplace.
7. Take "newcomer" jokes or pranks in stride.
8. Be friendly to everyone.
9. Give the job a fair chance.
10. Eat a balanced diet and get enough sleep.

Looking Right on the Job

Good Grooming

11. Keep yourself clean.
12. Put on clean underwear and socks every day.
13. Use a deodorant to help control body odor.
14. If you use cologne or aftershave, use only a little.
15. Keep your hair clean and trimmed.

16. Make sure your hands are clean and your nails are trimmed.
17. Keep your teeth clean and your breath fresh.
18. Women should use makeup carefully.
19. Men, keep your moustache or beard clean and well trimmed.

Dressing Right for Work

20. Dress as your co-workers dress.
21. Avoid wearing clothing fads to work.
22. Learn to choose clothes that fit well.
23. Buy work clothes that are easy to take care of.
24. Wear simple jewelry, if any.
25. Be sure your clothes are neat and clean.
26. Have good posture.
27. Try to always look your best at work.

Getting Along with Your Boss

28. Learn what's important to your boss.
29. Try to make your boss look good.
30. Accept jobs from your boss with a positive attitude.
31. Follow the boss's directions.
32. Learn to take criticism in stride.
33. Be loyal to your boss.
34. Be loyal to the company you work for.
35. Be willing to work!
36. Do your job the best you can.
37. Be a worker the boss knows he or she can depend on.
38. Obey the rules of the company.

Getting Along with Your Co-Workers

39. Do your share of the work.
40. Treat your co-workers with respect.
41. Listen to co-workers' ideas respectfully.
42. If you disagree with someone, do so in a calm, polite way.
43. Be a team player.

Friends at Work

44. Be interested in your co-workers.
45. Be considerate.
46. Be loyal to your co-workers.
47. Don't brag about how good you are.
48. Don't make a habit of borrowing money from your co-workers.
49. Don't complain all the time.
50. Praise your co-workers for their successes.
51. Don't take too long for coffee breaks or lunch breaks.
52. Choose your friends carefully when you start a new job.
53. Don't pick up bad habits in order to "fit in."
54. Stay away from "complainers."

Doing Your Best Work

55. Do more than is required of you.
56. Work until the job is done.
57. Be reliable.
58. Be orderly.
59. If you make a mistake, correct it quickly.
60. Use your time well.

61. Ask questions when you don't understand.
62. Take pride in your work.

Communication Skills

Speaking Skills

63. Speak clearly. Speak so others can hear you.
64. Avoid using slang and don't swear at work.
65. Don't interrupt when someone else is talking.
66. If someone compliments you, smile and say "thank you."
67. Don't try to cover up your mistakes.
68. Say "no" if asked to do something you think is wrong.
69. Learn to disagree with others in a pleasant way.
70. Don't whine and complain.
71. Make the other person glad he or she talked to you.

Listening Skills

72. Listen carefully when you're introduced to someone.
73. Listen when you're given directions.
74. Listen to learn what's going on around you at work.
75. Give the person speaking to you your full attention.
76. Make sure you understand what the other person is saying.

Using the Telephone at Work

77. Answer business phone calls on the first or second ring.
78. Answer the phone in a friendly, helpful manner.
79. Know how your boss wants you to answer the phone.
80. Make sure you get the caller's name right.

81. Learn to take good, complete phone messages.
82. Don't keep people waiting too long "on hold."
83. Keep a pleasant attitude on the phone.

Dealing with Customers

84. Greet each customer with a friendly smile.
85. If you're in sales, know your product or service well.
86. Treat customers as you would like to be treated.
87. Don't ignore customers or keep them waiting too long.
88. Handle customer complaints pleasantly.
89. Always thank the customer for coming in.

Problems at Work

Stress at Work

90. Exercise can help reduce stress.
91. A balanced diet helps you stand up to stress.
92. Enough sleep gives you energy to face the day.
93. Don't worry about things you can't control.
94. Do the most important jobs first.
95. Take time in your life to do something you enjoy.
96. Learn ways to relax.

Discrimination

97. You may choose to ignore *minor* remarks or slights.
98. Don't fight back on the same level.
99. Win the respect of others by doing your best work.
100. Get help to solve the problem if it is serious.

Sexual Harassment

101. Don't ignore it.
102. Keep a written report of exactly what happened.
103. Tell the person harassing you to stop.
104. If the harassment does not stop at once, tell your boss.
105. If the problem continues without help from higher management, you can contact the Equal Employment Opportunity Commission (EEOC).
106. The ACLU (American Civil Liberties Union) or a lawyer can also help you.

Romance in the Office

107. Save the romance for after work.
108. Remember that at work the job must come first.

The Office Party

109. Accept the party invitation if at all possible.
110. Go easy on the drinks and don't take drugs.
111. Avoid sexy or unusual clothing. And dress nicely.
112. Be sure to greet the boss and his or her family.
113. Avoid telling jokes that may offend others. And don't be too loud.
114. Thank your boss for a great time before you leave.

Crime in the Workplace

115. If you see a minor wrongdoing, you might let it go.
116. You might choose to speak to the person alone.
117. In serious cases, you need to tell the boss.

Quitting Your Job

118. Don't quit a good job just for a small pay raise.

119. Don't always compare your job with others.
120. Don't change jobs in too much of a hurry.
121. Don't quit in a huff based on one argument or problem.
122. Look for another job if you can't do the work.
123. Look around for another job if you're bored stiff.
124. Look around if you can't advance on your job.
125. Look around if you and your company are a "bad fit."
126. If you decide to quit, keep your old job until you have another.
127. Keep doing your best work until you leave your old job.
128. Leave behind a good image of yourself when you do leave.
129. Tell your boss you're quitting before you tell co-workers.
130. Give 2 weeks to 1 month notice.
131. Do what you can to help your replacement.

Getting Fired or Laid Off

132. Exit with class.
133. If you get fired, you were *fired*, you did not *quit*.
134. You should get some severance pay.
135. You should get paid for unused vacation time.
136. Try to find out why you were fired.
137. Find out if you can keep your health insurance for awhile.
138. Get a letter of recommendation.
139. Sign up for unemployment compensation.
140. Start looking for a new job quickly.

Getting Promotions and Raises

Getting a Promotion

141. Learn more about the company you work for.
142. Do your very best at the job you have now.
143. Check your work habits and attitude.
144. Set goals for yourself.
145. Make yourself *look* like a successful person.

How to Get a Raise

146. List the reasons you think you should get a raise.
147. Talk to your boss when you think he or she is in a good mood and not busy.
148. Keep your talk positive and businesslike.
149. Give your boss time to think it over.
150. If you're turned down, try to find out why.